MW01297918

The dark, the gloomy, and the beautiful.

somewhere in purgatory

theres a name for heaven and hell,
a reason for its existence,

but no one tells you
theres a place much worse,
where you're stuck between heaven and hell
and theres no reasoning.

they give you a diagnosis
and tell you theres something wrong

but no one tells them
purgatory is in your head
and you're lost somewhere inside it.

devour

i cannot feel

but the emptiness in my chest

is eating me alive

foxglove

night after night
you rummage through my mind.
unlocking memories i forgot i had.

you buried your roots
so far down,
that i cant remember how it felt
before you.

you hid behind innocence and beauty
as you destroyed the surrounding
thoughts.

i never realized flowers
could be poisonous
until i consumed what i thought was love,
and died still believing it was true.

how it feels to be loved

i found comfort in
words that were spoken,
and safety in your arms.

the reassurance in your voice
gave me goosebumps.

it was going to be different this time

growing closer and closer
like vines on a wall,
intertwining with similarities
and hope.

love was written all over my face,
written the way i thought matched yours

it was supposed to be different this time

but before i knew it,
you were

g o n e.

conundrum

a loss for words

swollen tongue
and a rock filled throat

eyes stinging from
too many tears

it was supposed to be different,

i was supposed to be different.

you grow,
as i rot.

poisonous,
yet still so inviting.

would i have done it all over again?

if my words had been lost when you found me,
maybe my heart would still beat.

do over

maybe it would have been different

maybe my heart wouldn’t hurt

maybe my heart wouldn’t hope

maybe i could have a proper goodbye

maybe i could receive closure

maybe seeing you one last time would be enough

but maybe

i would do it all over again.

fallen

i saw an angel in your eyes
preaching about love
and salvation.

i lost sight of my purpose,
my meaning,
my will.

i began to look closer,
you were so convincing

you could've fooled god,
you could've been the devil,

but you weren't the angel who fell,

i was.

it was just a dream

everything was how i remembered,
from the position of buildings,
to cracks in the pavement,
i was back.

my first thought
was to find you.

having no recollection of how i arrived,
trying to remember what occurred before this,

none of it was real.

hurting myself to convince myself otherwise
meant speaking to you.

the anxiety consumed me,
i was fearful even in here.

the world as you knew it

I've been screaming in an bottomless abyss for almost a decade
some days, i hope i'll hear a returning voice,
most days, the silence is deafening.
the darkness scared me,
never knowing what was waiting for me at the bottom,
but the world behind me keeps creeping up closer and closer,
the emptiness becomes inviting after some time.
i hope for the day i let it consume me.
i fear i won't be able to turn around and face the world
when i fall back into the comfort of
nothingness.

how it feels to be loved

the warmth coming from
the decorations on my skin,
felt nostalgic.

i've been here countless times,

i'm not sure any pure skin
is left.

too many bruises,
scars,
memories...

they are permanently stitched
into every cell.

surprised by the throbbing
in my chest.

i forget it exist.

then again,
i forget i do too.

tainted heart

all our lives
we fight to find love,

but when we find it,
it no longer feels like enough.

stargazing

you hope the constellations on your skin
will distract them from seeing the stars dying
in your eyes.

all hallows' eve

once a year,
we dress up to
become someone,
something,
we’ve always wanted to be.

this year i will treat myself
into being your lover,

and trick myself into believing it
was real.

the fear of being loved

i don't expect you to understand
how my skin crawls when presented with
affection.

i never learned to enjoy the moment
because it was meant to end,
eventually.

my heart hardens
as its temperature drops,

"it's for the best."
rolls off my tongue in a knee-jerk reaction.

i fought too long and too hard.
i don't have it in me anymore.

paradox

i had the basis of my life all wrong.
the people, the feelings...
i was searching for a meaning in an endless black hole.
broken promise after broken promise
the system in my brain overheated to the point of no return.
the comfort i suddenly feel in the dark is melancholic.
it all leads back to the nothingness,
the emptiness.
and that's what my life is,

a void in time that should not exist.

different memories, same pain

you say you’re used to it
but we both know

it hurts just as much as the
first.

storm season

it’s hard to feel hopeful now a days.
when everything is changing and disappearing.
daily storms and rain clouds perfectly describe
the war going on in my mind.

while the outside world is preparing for devastation,
it’s hard to see the sunlight
even when it’s blinding you.

sometimes i never see the end of the storm.
surprised when the sun shines,
because i’m used to the gloomy hues.

it’s hard to feel hopeful —
it’s hard to feel.

even when the clouds disappear
and the sky turns bright blue,
i’ll look for the comfort of gray
and wish to hear the thunder roaring.

puppet

my body feels attached to strings.
forcing me to stay up,
never letting me rest.

my mind is dark and barren.
no residual hope hiding in small cracks.

my heart feels vacant
sometimes, i’m not sure if it still beats.

porcelain doll

decorated for the pleasure of others,

put together for everyone else but never for myself.

fake smile and lively eyes painted on with a sparkle.

long limbs that makes all the rest come together delicately.

displays of admiration for a body that holds me captive.

they see me when they need convenience, otherwise,

i am left on the shelf collecting dust

with only my hollowness, my fragility, and the cold of my skin.

mental prison

in solitary confinement,
i lose sight

of my hope,
my will,
my power.

these thoughts are their own,

forming into people
from the past

they unplug every lamp,
break every bulb,
and block out whatever light that is left

they feed on darkness,
they hurt from light,
they leave me alone,

as long as i stay in the dark.

rebirth

the infection in the walls that imprison me,
have finally ignited.
i watch as i dropped the match;
starting a war that needed to be fought.

you planted a seed of hatred in my mind
and sat back as it infested everything around me.

i was a fly in the web i helped you spin,
a pawn in a game i never had a chance of winning until,
the flames started growing.

as the house was swallowed by orange and red,
memories seared into my skin,

the ashes decorated the floor
like confetti —

maybe, now, new life may grow.

the sun will still rise in the morning

sometimes you need to escape.
not based, exclusively, on one reason —
it's night and day, really.

you cant stop the sun from rising
or diminish the moons light.

the day will go on,
the dark will swallow things whole

but thats not what we escape from.
we want to leave who we are,
who we think we are.

that chance,
that decision to leave or
temporarily forget,
is inevitable.

don’t allow that to change
your destination.

at times, we stumble upon the unknown.
at one point, we were apart of that.
it may feel that we still reside in the nothingness
but don’t escape to the past
that is who, or what, we are running from.

CPSIA information can be obtained
at www.ICGtesting.com
Printed in the USA
LVHW040127080621
689672LV00005B/233